eltic Letters & Ornaments

CD-ROM AND BOOK

Dover Publications, Inc., Mineola, New York

The CD-ROM in this book contains all of the images. There is no installation necessary. Just insert the CD into your computer and call the images into your favorite software (refer to the documentation with your software for further instructions). Each image has been scanned at 600 dpi and saved in six different formats—BMP, EPS, GIF, JPEG, PICT, and TIFF. The JPEG and GIF files—the most popular graphics file types used on the Web—are Internet ready.

The "Images" folder on the CD contains a number of different folders. All of the TIFF images have been placed in one folder, as have all of the PICT, all of the EPS, etc. The images in each of these folders are identical except for file format. Every image has a unique file name in the following format: xxx.xxx. The first 3 or 4 characters of the file name, before the period, correspond to the number printed with the image in the book. The last 3 characters of the file name, after the period, refer to the file format. So, 001.TIF would be the first file in the TIFF folder.

Also included on the CD-ROM is Dover Design Manager, a simple graphics editing program for Windows that will allow you to view, print, crop, and rotate the images.

For technical support, contact:
Telephone: 1 (617) 249-0245
Fax: 1 (617) 249-0245
Email: dover@artimaging.com
Internet: **http://www.dovertechsupport.com**
The fastest way to receive technical support is via email or the Internet.

Bibliographical Note

Celtic Letters and Ornaments CD-ROM and Book is a new work, first published by Dover Publications, Inc., in 2007.

Dover Electronic Clip Art®

International Standard Book Number
ISBN-13: 978-0-486-99880-0
ISBN-10: 0-486-99880-0

Manufactured in the United States of America
Dover Publications, Inc., 31 East 2nd Street, Mineola, N.Y. 11501

001

002

003

004

005

006

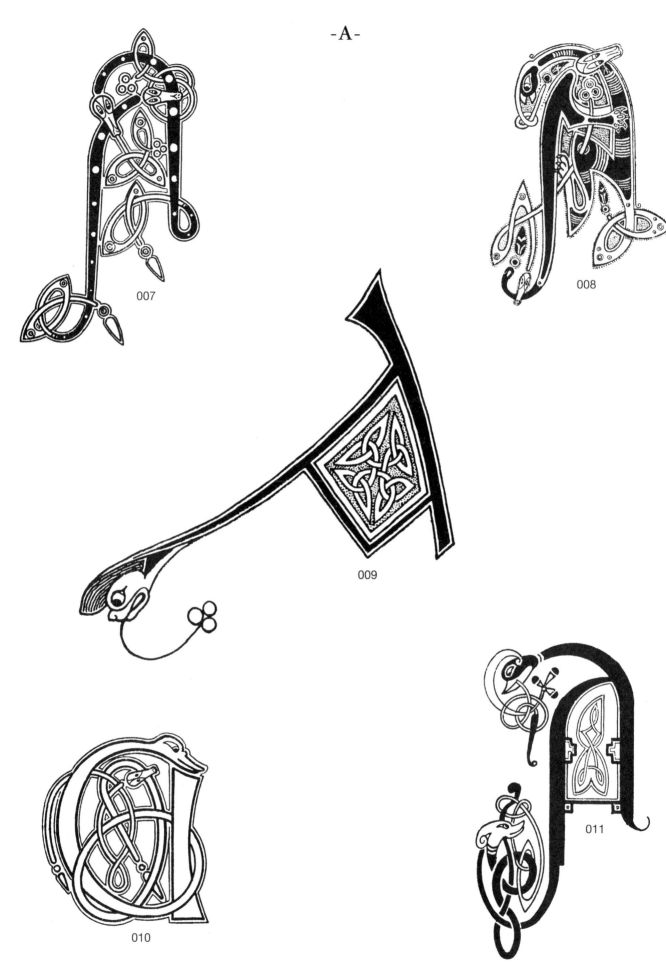

007

008

009

010

011

012

013

014

015

016

017

018

019

020

021

022

023

024

025

026

027

028

029

030

031

032

033

034

035

036

037

038

039

040

041

042   043   044

045

046

047

048

049

050

051

052

053

054

055

056

057

058

059

060

061

062

063

064

065

066

067

068

069

070

071

072

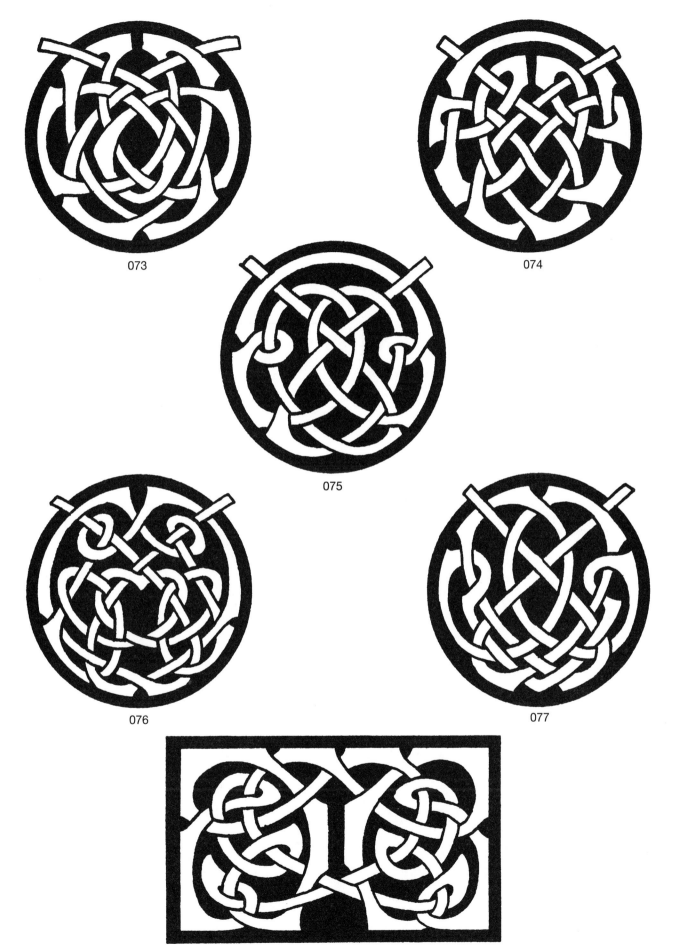

073

074

075

076

077

078

15

079

080

081

082

083

084

085

086

087

088

089

090

091

092

093

094

095

096

097

098

099

100

101

102

103

104

105

106

107

108

109

110

111

112

113

114

115

116

117

118

119

120

121

122

123

124

125

126

127

128

129

130

131

132

133

134

135

136

137

138

139

140

141

142

143

144

145

146

29

147

148

149

150

151

152

153

154

155

156

157

159

158

160

161

162

163

164

166

165

167

169

168

170

171

172

173

174

175

177

176

178

179

180

37

181

182

183

184

185

186

187

39

40

188

189

190

191

41

192

193

194

195

196

197

198

199

200   201   202   203

204   205   206

207   208   209   210

211   212   213

214   215   216

217   218   219   220

221   222   223

224   225   226   227